How do I put it on?

How do I put it on?

Shigeo Watanabe
Illustrated by Yasuo Ohtomo

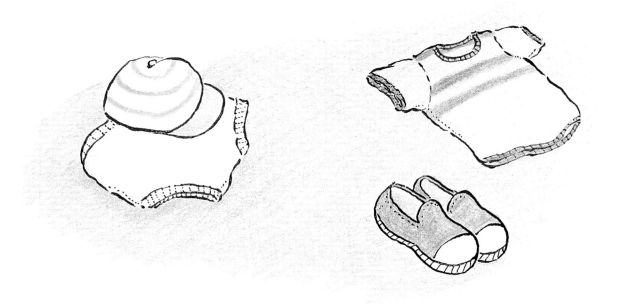

RED FOX

This is my shirt.

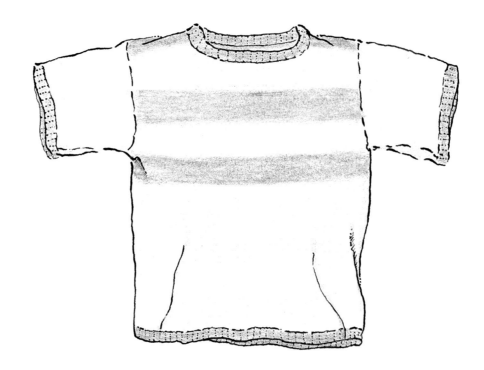

Do I put it on like this?

No!

I put my shirt over my head.

These are my pants.

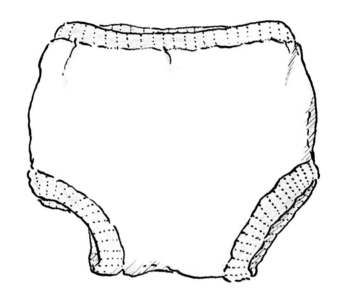

Do I put them on like this?

No!

I put my legs through my pants.

This is my cap.

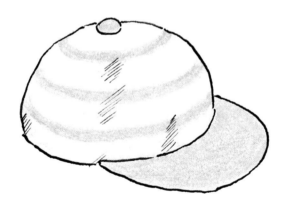

Do I put it on like this?

No!

I put my cap on my head.

These are my shoes.

Do I put them on like this?

No!

I put my shoes on my feet.

Here goes . . .

Shirt.

Pants.

Cap.

Shoes.

I'm ready. Off I go!

A Red Fox Book

Published by Random House Children's Books
20 Vauxhall Bridge Road, London SW1V 2SA

A division of Random House UK Ltd
London Melbourne Sydney Auckland
Johannesburg and agencies throughout the world

First published in Tokyo by Fukuinkan Shoten 1977
First published in Great Britain by The Bodley Head Ltd. 1979

Red Fox edition 1993

7 9 10 8 6

Text © Shigeo Watanabe 1977
Illustrations © Yasuo Ohtomo 1977
English text © The Bodley Head 1979

Printed in China

ISBN 0 09 999940 4

Some bestselling Red Fox picture books

THE BIG ALFIE AND ANNIE ROSE STORYBOOK
by Shirley Hughes
OLD BEAR
by Jane Hissey
OI! GET OFF OUR TRAIN
by John Burningham
DON'T DO THAT!
by Tony Ross
NOT NOW, BERNARD
by David McKee
ALL JOIN IN
by Quentin Blake
THE WHALES' SONG
by Gary Blythe and Dyan Sheldon
JESUS' CHRISTMAS PARTY
by Nicholas Allan
THE PATCHWORK CAT
by Nicola Bayley and William Mayne
MATILDA
by Hilaire Belloc and Posy Simmonds
WILLY AND HUGH
by Anthony Browne
THE WINTER HEDGEHOG
by Ann and Reg Cartwright
A DARK, DARK TALE
by Ruth Brown
HARRY, THE DIRTY DOG
by Gene Zion and Margaret Bloy Graham
DR XARGLE'S BOOK OF EARTHLETS
by Jeanne Willis and Tony Ross
WHERE'S THE BABY?
by Pat Hutchins